Cargo Ships

by Adele D. Richardson

Bridgestone Books

an imprint of Capstone Press
Mankato, Minnesota

Bridgestone Books are published by Capstone Press
151 Good Counsel Drive, P.O. Box 669, Mankato, Minnesota 56002
http://www.capstone-press.com

Library of Congress Cataloging-in-Publication Data
Richardson, Adele D., 1966–
  Cargo ships/by Adele D. Richardson.
  p. cm.—(The transportation library)
  Includes bibliographical references and index.
  Summary: Describes early models, major parts, and the workings of cargo ships.
  ISBN 0-7368-0606-7
  1. Cargo ships—Juvenile literature. [1. Cargo ships.] I. Title. II. Series.
VM391 .R497 2001
623.8'245—dc21   00-022824

Editorial Credits
Karen L. Daas, editor; Timothy Halldin, cover designer and illustrator;
  Kimberly Danger and Heidi Schoof, photo researchers

Photo Credits
Archive Photos, 4, 12, 14, 16
Index Stock Imagery/Tina Buckman, 6–7
International Stock/T.M. Collins, cover; Scott Barrow, 18–19; Frank Grant, 20
Mary Messenger, 10

Bridgestone Books thanks Michele Higgins at the Port of Bellingham for reviewing this text.

1 2 3 4 5 6 06 05 04 03 02 01

Table of Contents

Cargo Ships

Cargo ships are large boats that transport cargo from one place to another. Most cargo ships travel on oceans. Some cargo ships can carry many types of cargo at one time. Other ships are built to carry one type of cargo.

cargo
goods that are transported
from one place to another

Parts of a Cargo Ship

A cargo ship has a large hull. Part of the hull holds the cargo ship's engines. The cargo ship's crew places cargo in the hull and on the deck. Cargo ships have a superstructure. The captain steers the ship from this building. The crew also can sleep there.

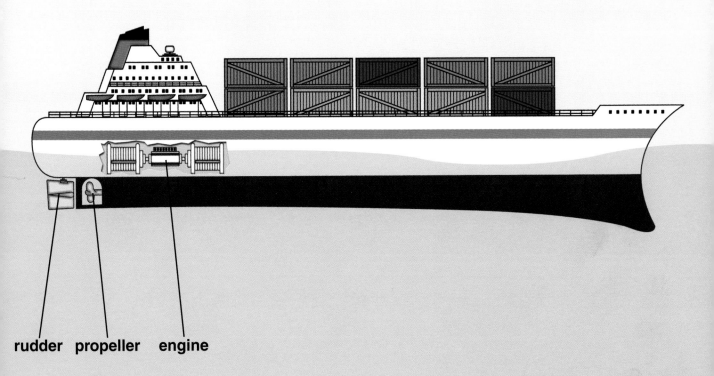

rudder **propeller** **engine**

How a Cargo Ship Works

A cargo ship uses diesel oil for fuel.
The fuel powers the cargo ship's
engine. The engine turns a propeller.
The propeller moves the cargo ship.
A rudder turns the cargo ship.

rudder

a plate on the back of a boat;
the captain uses a rudder to
turn a cargo ship.

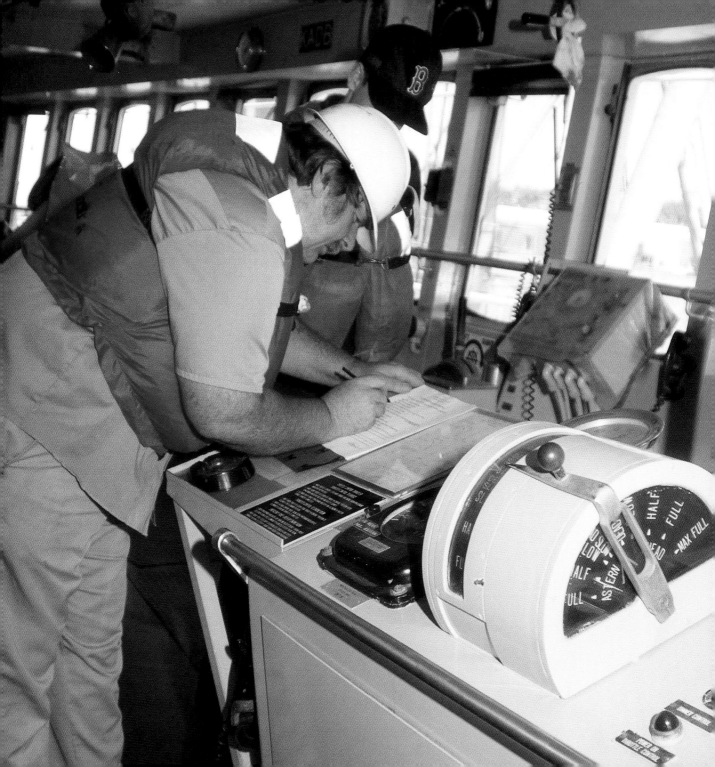

Steering a Cargo Ship

The captain steers a cargo ship from the bridge. This area is at the top of the ship's superstructure. The captain uses a computer to steer the cargo ship. The computer controls the direction and speed of the cargo ship. The computer also shows the ship's position in the ocean.

Invention of the Ship

Egyptians built some of the earliest ships from wood about 5,000 years ago. Wind captured in sails powered these ships. Egyptians used oars to steer the ships. They later added more sails and rudders to sailing ships. Sailors could control the ships better with these added parts.

Early Cargo Ships

Europeans invented the caravel. These wooden ships had three or four masts. Christopher Columbus sailed a caravel to North America in 1492. Europeans later invented clipper ships. These long, narrow ships traveled quickly over the ocean.

mast

a pole that stands on the deck of a ship and supports sails

Later Cargo Ships

In 1838, Isambard Kingdom Brunel built the first iron cargo ship. He then built the *Great Eastern* in 1860. In 1865, this ship laid the first telegraph cable that crossed the Atlantic Ocean. This cable allowed the United States and Europe to send telegraph messages to each other.

telegraph
a system for sending messages over long distances

Cargo Ships Today

Today, companies transport many types of goods on cargo ships. Workers put some cargo in containers. Crews use a crane to lower these boxes into the cargo ship's hull and onto the deck. Bulk cargo ships carry goods such as wheat and sugar. Tanker cargo ships transport oil.

Cargo Ship Facts

- Some bulk cargo ships carry coal. Workers use high-speed belts to load the coal. The coal is loaded into large separate areas. Workers cover each area once it is full.

- A cargo ship that carries cars and trucks is called a ro-ro. The vehicles roll on and roll off the cargo ship.

- Most cargo ships are 600 to 900 feet (183 to 274 meters) long. Some cargo ships are more than 1,500 feet (457 meters) long. Workers sometimes ride bicycles to get from one end of the cargo ship to the other.

- Refrigerator ships carry meat and fruit. These cargo ships keep food cold so it does not spoil.

Hands On: Build a Soap-Powered Boat

All cargo ships need fuel to move through water. You can build a model boat and power it with soap.

What You Need

One index card
Scissors
A large baking dish
Water
Liquid dish soap

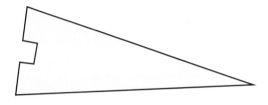

What You Do

1. Carefully cut the index card into a long triangle about 3 inches (7.6 centimeters) long and 1 inch (2.5 centimeters) wide at the base.
2. Cut a small square into the shortest side of the triangle. This triangle is your boat. Your boat should look like the shape shown above.
3. Fill the baking dish with water.
4. Place your boat gently on the surface of the water.
5. Squeeze a drop of liquid dish soap into the small square.

The soap will act like fuel. Your boat will move across the water. Before doing this experiment again, rinse the baking dish. If soap is left in the water, the boat will not move.

Words To Know

container (kuhn-TAYN-er)—a type of box that can be loaded onto a cargo ship; containers can hold many types of goods.

hull (HUHL)—the main body of a cargo ship

propeller (pruh-PEL-ur)—a set of spinning blades that moves a cargo ship through water

rudder (RUHD-ur)—a plate on the back of a boat; the rudder turns a cargo ship.

superstructure (SOO-per-struhk-chur)—a building on a cargo ship; the sleeping quarters and bridge are in the superstructure.

transport (transs-PORT)—to move people or goods from one place to another

Read More

Cooper, Jason. *Cargo Ships.* Boats and Ships. Vero Beach, Fla.: Rourke, 1999.

Maynard, Christopher. *The Usborne Book of Cutaway Boats.* London: Usborne Publishing, 1996.

Royston, Angela. *Boats and Ships.* Inside and Out. Des Plaines, Ill.: Heinemann Interactive Library, 1998.

Internet Sites

BoatSafeKids
http://www.boatsafe.com/kids/index.htm
National Maritime Museum
http://www.nmm.ac.uk/galleries/cargoes.html
Sea Vehicles
http://www.transport-pf.or.jp/english/sea/cargo/kind1.html

Index